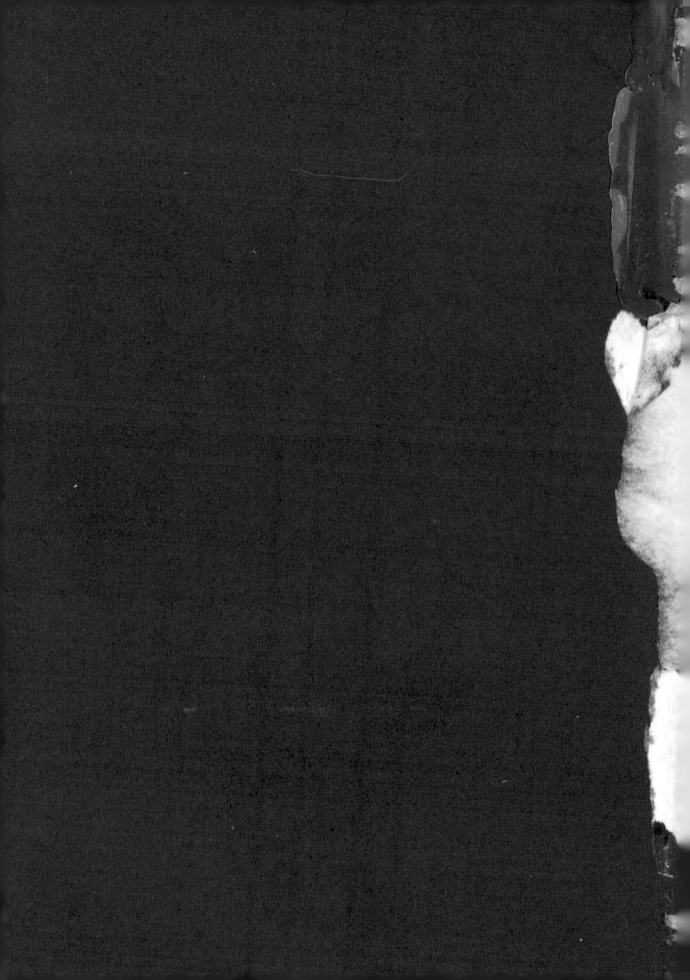

Published 2024

FiNGERPRINT!

An imprint of Prakash Books India Pvt. Ltd

113/A, Darya Ganj,
New Delhi-110 002
Email: info@prakashbooks.com/sales@prakashbooks.com

 Fingerprint Publishing
 @FingerprintP
 @fingerprintpublishingbooks

ISBN: 978 93 5856 731 1

TO ....

FROM ....

Courage is not the absence of fear but rather the strength to face it head-on. It is not a distant ideal but a living, breathing force that resides within us all. It is the fuel that transforms the ordinary into the extraordinary.

Courage is not reserved for a chosen few. It begins with small acts of bravery, and with each step, it grows, and our capacity to face the world expands.

If you find yourself standing at the edge of a challenge, embrace courage as your unwavering ally in the fight against adversities!

"COURAGE IS CONTAGIOUS.
WHEN A BRAVE MAN TAKES A
STAND, THE SPINES OF OTHERS
ARE OFTEN STIFFENED."

BILLY GRAHAM

**"BE BRAVE. TAKE RISKS.
NOTHING CAN
SUBSTITUTE EXPERIENCE."**

PAULO COELHO

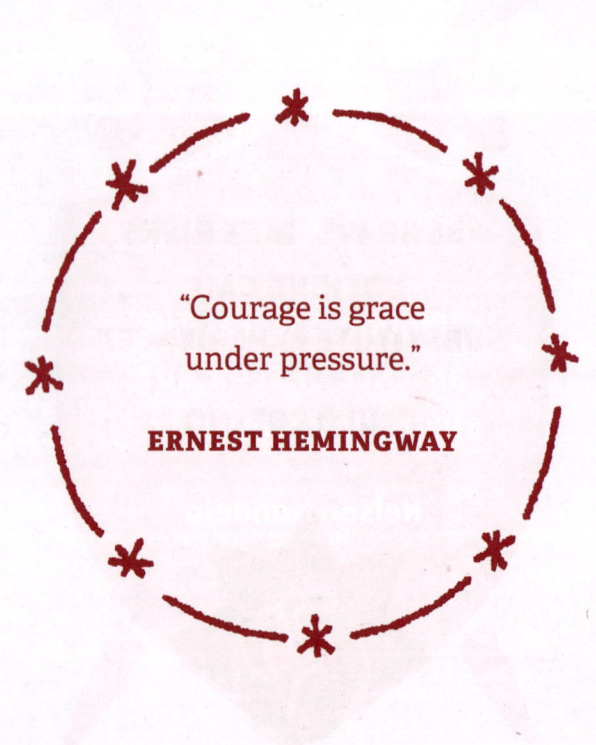

"Courage is grace
under pressure."

ERNEST HEMINGWAY

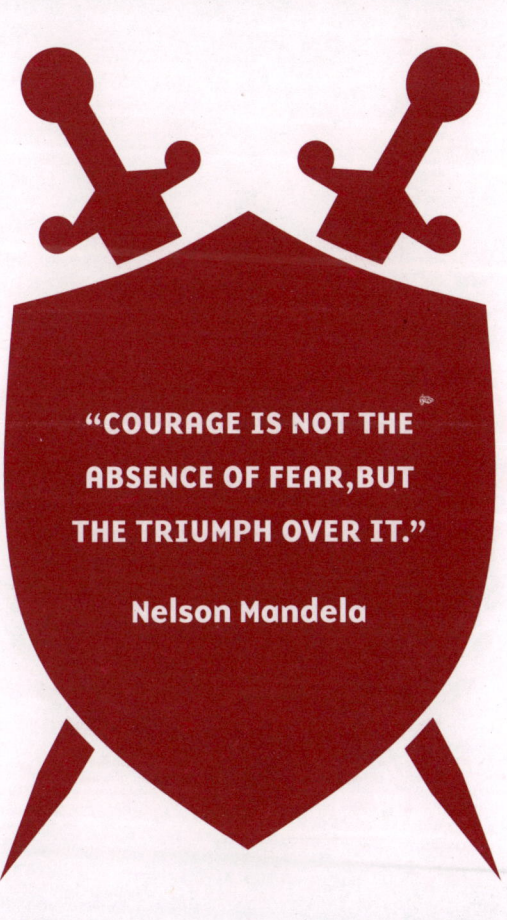

"COURAGE IS NOT THE ABSENCE OF FEAR, BUT THE TRIUMPH OVER IT."

Nelson Mandela

"ONE MAN WITH COURAGE

IS THE MAJORITY."

THOMAS JEFFERSON

"The greatest test of courage
on the earth is to bear
defeat without losing heart."

ROBERT GREEN
INGERSOLL

"COURAGE IS THE KEY THAT UNLOCKS YOUR POTENTIAL."

Roy T. Bennett

"Courage is the fuel that allows ordinary people to achieve extraordinary results."

JON GORDON

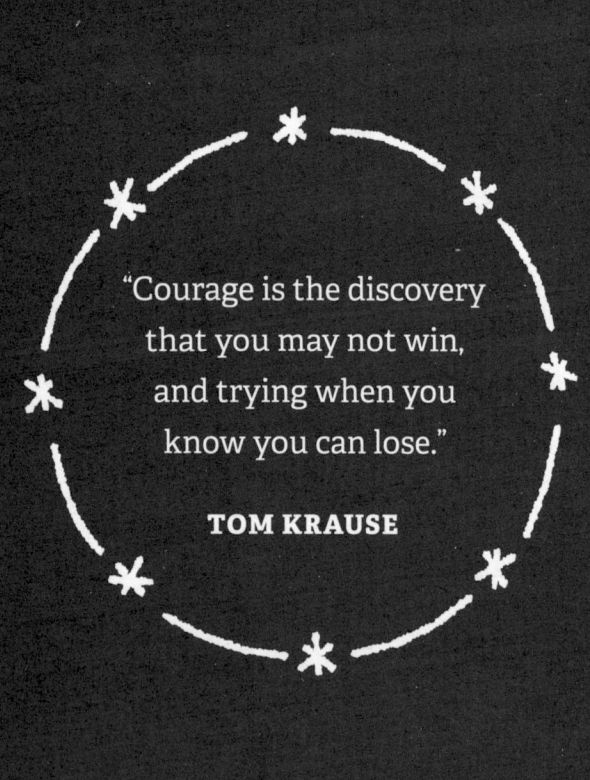

"Courage is the discovery
that you may not win,
and trying when you
know you can lose."

TOM KRAUSE

"**KNOWLEDGE WITHOUT COURAGE IS STERILE.**"

BALTASAR GRACIÁN

"Courage is not the towering
oak that sees storms
come and go; it is the
fragile blossom that
opens in the snow."

ALICE M. SWAIM

"COURAGE IS KNOWING
WHAT NOT TO FEAR."

PLATO

"KEEP YOUR FEARS TO YOURSELF, BUT SHARE YOUR COURAGE WITH OTHERS."

ROBERT LOUIS STEVENSON

"BRAVERY IS BEING
THE ONLY ONE WHO
KNOWS YOU'RE AFRAID."

FRANKLIN P. JONES

"Success is not final,
failure is not fatal:
It is the courage to
continue that counts."

WINSTON CHURCHILL

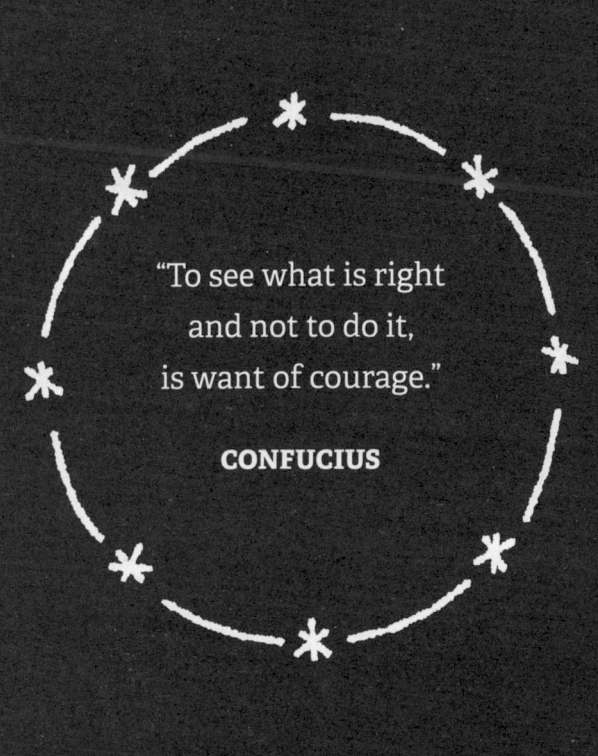

"To see what is right
and not to do it,
is want of courage."

CONFUCIUS

"COURAGE IS THE PRICE
THAT LIFE EXACTS
FOR GRANTING PEACE."

Amelia Earhart

"Courage is the most important of all the virtues because without courage, you can't practice any other virtue consistently."

MAYA ANGELOU

"He who is not courageous
enough to take risks will
accomplish nothing in life."

MUHAMMAD ALI

"Courage is not the absence
of despair; it is rather the
capacity to move ahead
in spite of despair."

ROLLO MAY

"SCARED IS WHAT YOU'RE FEELING. BRAVE IS WHAT YOU'RE DOING."

EMMA DONOGHUE

"THE OPPOSITE OF COURAGE
IS NOT COWARDICE;
IT IS CONFORMITY.
EVEN A DEAD FISH CAN
GO WITH THE FLOW."

JIM HIGHTOWER

"COURAGE IS FOUND
IN UNLIKELY PLACES."

J.R.R. TOLKIEN

"Bravery is the capacity
to perform properly even
when scared half to death."

OMAR N. BRADLEY

"COURAGE IS NOT ABOUT
NOT BEING SCARED
BUT THE TRIUMPH OVER IT."

Ruth Gordon

"COURAGE IS NOT SIMPLY
ONE OF THE VIRTUES BUT
THE FORM OF EVERY VIRTUE
AT THE TESTING POINT."

C.S. LEWIS

"IF YOU COULD GET
THE COURAGE TO BEGIN,
YOU HAVE THE COURAGE
TO SUCCEED."

DAVID VISCOTT

"COURAGE IS THE ART
OF BEING THE ONLY ONE
WHO KNOWS YOU'RE
SCARED TO DEATH."

EARL WILSON

"Courage is the greatest of
all virtues because if you
haven't courage, you may
not have an opportunity
to use any of the others."

SAMUEL JOHNSON

"IF YOU ARE LUCKY ENOUGH TO
FIND A WAY OF LIFE YOU LOVE,
YOU HAVE TO FIND THE
COURAGE TO LIVE IT."

JOHN IRVING

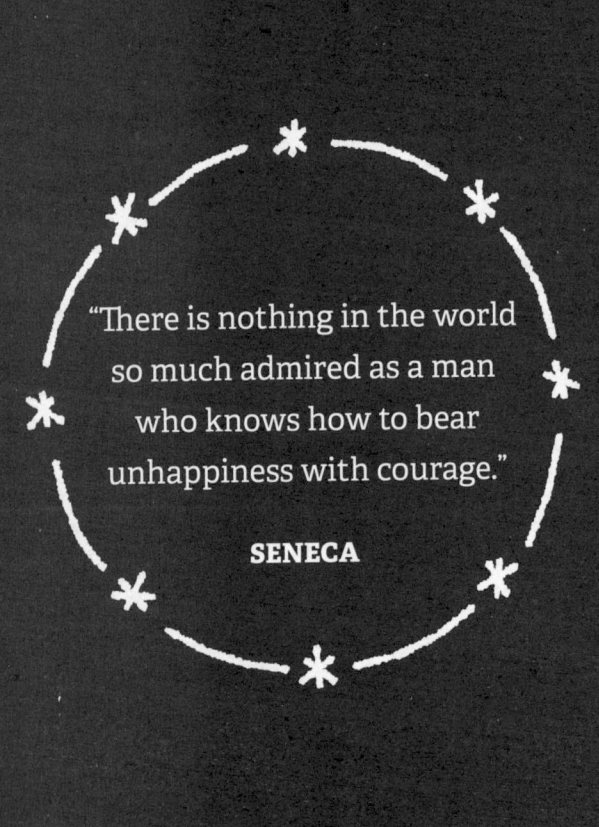

"There is nothing in the world
so much admired as a man
who knows how to bear
unhappiness with courage."

SENECA

"COURAGE IS DOING WHAT
YOU'RE AFRAID TO DO.
THERE CAN BE NO COURAGE
UNLESS YOU'RE SCARED."

EDDIE RICKENBACKER

"Courage is resistance to
fear, mastery of fear,
not absence of fear."

MARK TWAIN

"Courage is not limited to the battlefield bravely catching a thief in your house. The real tests of courage are much quieter. They are the inner tests, like remaining faithful when nobody's looking, like enduring pain when the room is empty, like standing alone when you're misunderstood."

CHARLES SWINDOLL

"IT TAKES COURAGE TO GROW UP AND BECOME WHO YOU REALLY ARE."

E.E. CUMMINGS

"THE SECRET TO HAPPINESS
IS FREEDOM, AND THE SECRET
TO FREEDOM IS COURAGE."

THUCYDIDES

"Courage doesn't always roar. Sometimes courage is the little voice at the end of the day that says 'I'll try again tomorrow.'"

MARY ANNE RADMACHER

"COURAGE IS THE POWER
TO LET GO OF THE FAMILIAR."

Raymond Lindquist

"LIFE SHRINKS OR EXPANDS
IN PROPORTION TO
ONE'S COURAGE."

ANAÏS NIN

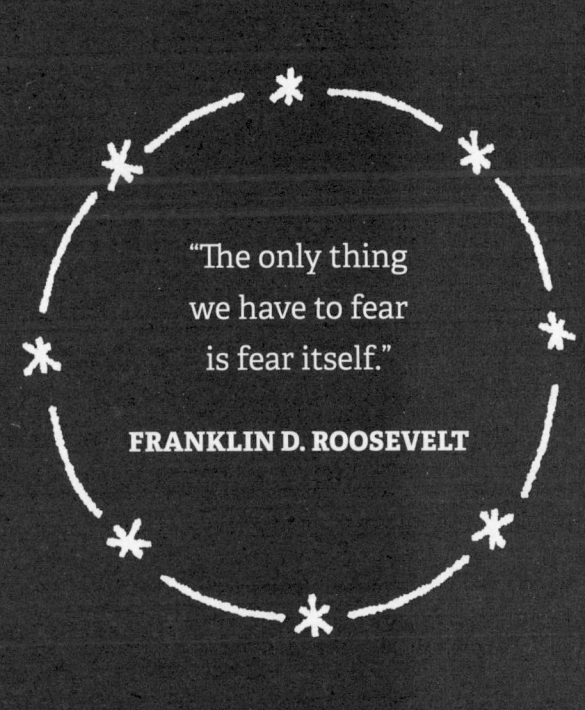

"The only thing
we have to fear
is fear itself."

FRANKLIN D. ROOSEVELT

"THE DESIRE FOR SAFETY STANDS AGAINST EVERY GREAT AND NOBLE ENTERPRISE."

TACITUS

"COURAGE IS NOT WAITING FOR THE STORM TO PASS, BUT LEARNING TO DANCE IN THE RAIN."

Vivian Greene

"You cannot swim
for new horizons until
you have courage to
lose sight of the shore."

WILLIAM FAULKNER

"COURAGE IS NOT WAITING FOR THE STORM TO PASS, BUT LEARNING TO DANCE IN THE RAIN."

Vivian Greene

"You cannot swim
for new horizons until
you have courage to
lose sight of the shore."

WILLIAM FAULKNER

"Bravery is the choice to show up and listen to another person, be it a loved one or perceived foe, even when it is uncomfortable, painful, or the last thing you want to do."

ALARIC HUTCHINSON

"COURAGE RESULTS WHEN
ONE'S CONVICTIONS
ARE BIGGER THAN
ONE'S FEARS."

ORRIN WOODWARD

"THE MOST COURAGEOUS ACT IS STILL TO THINK FOR YOURSELF."

COCO CHANEL

WHY SHOULD YOU BE BRAVE?

✳ It enables us to step outside our comfort zone and embrace new experiences, which is vital for personal growth.

✳ With bravery, we can transform obstacles into stepping stones towards success.

✳ By being brave, we inspire those around us. Our actions demonstrate that it is possible to overcome fears and obstacles, motivating others to embrace their own courage.

✳ Being brave means embracing authenticity and staying true to ourselves. It allows us to express our thoughts, feelings, and values without fear of judgment.

"Believe in yourself.
You are braver than
you think, more talented than
you know, and capable of
more than you imagine."

ROY T. BENNETT

"COURAGE STARTS WITH
SHOWING UP AND LETTING
OURSELVES BE SEEN."

BRENÉ BROWN

"WHAT WOULD LIFE BE
IF WE HAD NO COURAGE
TO ATTEMPT ANYTHING?"

VINCENT VAN GOGH

"WITH ENOUGH COURAGE,
YOU CAN DO WITHOUT
A REPUTATION."

Margaret Mitchell

"TO HAVE COURAGE FOR
WHATEVER COMES IN LIFE,
EVERYTHING LIES IN THAT."

SAINT TERESA OF ÁVILA

"Real courage is when you know
you're licked before you begin,
but you begin anyway and
see it through no matter what."

HARPER LEE

"YOU WILL NEVER DO ANYTHING IN THIS WORLD WITHOUT COURAGE. IT IS THE GREATEST QUALITY OF THE MIND NEXT TO HONOR."

ARISTOTLE

"CREATIVITY TAKES COURAGE."

HENRI MATISSE

"COURAGE ISN'T HAVING
THE STRENGTH TO GO ON,
IT IS GOING ON WHEN YOU
DON'T HAVE STRENGTH."

NAPOLEON BONAPARTE

"THE BRAVE MAN IS NOT HE
WHO DOES NOT FEEL AFRAID
BUT HE WHO
CONQUERS THAT FEAR."

NELSON MANDELA

"THE BEST PROTECTION
ANY WOMAN CAN HAVE . . .
IS COURAGE."

ELIZABETH CADY STANTON

"YOU DON'T HAVE TO BE RICH TO BE GENEROUS, AND YOU DON'T HAVE TO BE FEARLESS TO BE BRAVE."

Kevin Heath

"Courage is a special kind of knowledge: the knowledge of how to fear what ought to be feared and how not to fear what ought not to be feared."

DAVID BEN-GURION

"IT TAKES A LOT OF COURAGE
TO SHOW YOUR DREAMS
TO SOMEONE ELSE."

ERMA BOMBECK

"Failure is unimportant.
It takes courage to make
a fool of yourself."

CHARLIE CHAPLIN

"Have courage for the great
sorrows of life and patience for
the small ones; and when you
have laboriously accomplished
your daily task, go to sleep
in peace. God is awake."

VICTOR HUGO

"Have the courage to follow your heart and intuition. They somehow already know what you truly want to become. Everything else is secondary."

STEVE JOBS

"FROM CARING COMES COURAGE."

LAO TZU

"I would define true courage
to have a perfect sensibility
of the measure of danger, and
a mental willingness to endure it."

**WILLIAM TECUMSEH
SHERMAN**

"CLEAR THINKING
REQUIRES COURAGE
RATHER THAN INTELLIGENCE."

THOMAS SZASZ

"HE IS A MAN OF COURAGE
WHO DOES NOT RUN AWAY
BUT REMAINS AT HIS POST AND
FIGHTS AGAINST THE ENEMY."

SOCRATES

"COURAGE IS ON DISPLAY
EVERY DAY, AND ONLY THE
COURAGEOUS WRING
THE MOST OUT OF LIFE."

ZIG ZIGLAR

"PHYSICAL BRAVERY IS
AN ANIMAL INSTINCT;
MORAL BRAVERY IS
MUCH HIGHER AND
TRUER COURAGE."

WENDELL PHILLIPS

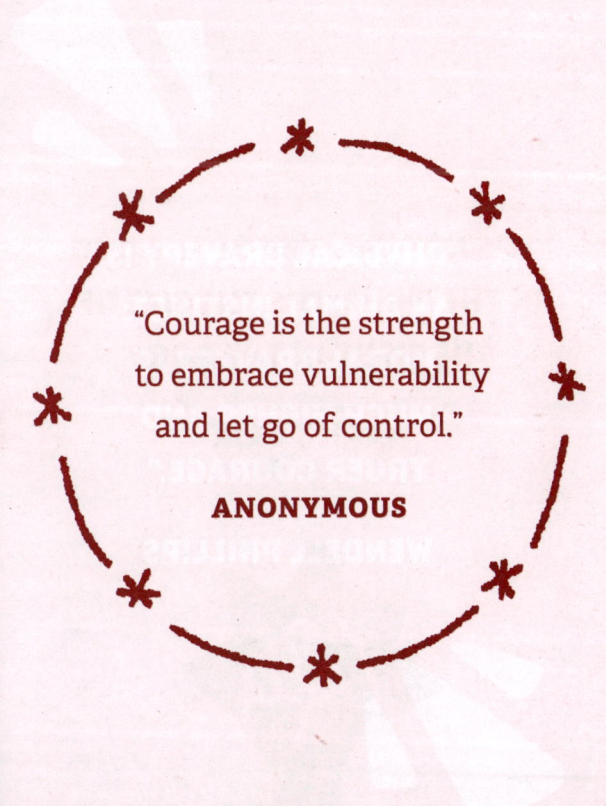

"Courage is the strength to embrace vulnerability and let go of control."

ANONYMOUS

"IT'S NOT THE SIZE OF THE DOG IN THE FIGHT; IT'S THE SIZE OF THE FIGHT IN THE DOG."

MARK TWAIN

"COURAGE IS THE COMPLEMENT
OF FEAR. A MAN WHO IS
FEARLESS CANNOT
BE COURAGEOUS.
HE IS ALSO A FOOL."

ROBERT A. HEINLEIN

"Courage to me is doing something daring, no matter how afraid, insecure, intimidated, alone, unworthy, incapable, ridiculed or whatever other paralyzing emotion you might feel. Courage is taking action . . . no matter what. So you're afraid? Be afraid. Be scared silly to the point you're trembling and nauseous, but do it anyway!"

RICHELLE E. GOODRICH

"THERE IS A STUBBORNNESS
ABOUT ME THAT NEVER CAN
BEAR TO BE FRIGHTENED
AT THE WILL OF OTHERS.
MY COURAGE ALWAYS RISES
AT EVERY ATTEMPT TO
INTIMIDATE ME."

JANE AUSTEN

"Inaction breeds doubt and fear.
Action breeds confidence
and courage. If you want to
conquer fear, do not sit home
and think about it.
Go out and get busy."

DALE CARNEGIE

"EVERYONE HAS TALENT.
WHAT'S RARE IS THE COURAGE
TO FOLLOW IT TO THE DARK
PLACES WHERE IT LEADS."

ERICA JONG

"THE BIGGEST ADVENTURE
YOU CAN EVER TAKE IS TO LIVE
THE LIFE OF YOUR DREAMS."

Oprah Winfrey

"Real courage is doing the right
thing when nobody's looking.
Doing the unpopular thing
because it's what you believe,
and to heck with everybody."

JUSTIN CRONIN

"PRIDE IS HOLDING YOUR HEAD UP WHEN EVERYONE AROUND YOU HAVE THEIRS BOWED. COURAGE IS WHAT MAKES YOU DO IT."

BRYCE COURTENAY

"Great occasions do not make heroes
or cowards; they simply unveil them to
the eyes of men. Silently and perceptibly,
as we wake or sleep, we grow strong
or weak; and last, some crisis shows
what we have become."

BROOKE FOSS WESTCOTT

"Confront the dark parts of yourself,
and work to banish them with
illumination and forgiveness.
Your willingness to wrestle with
your demons will cause
your angels to sing."

AUGUST WILSON

"HE WHO JUMPS INTO
THE VOID OWES NO
EXPLANATION TO THOSE
WHO STAND AND WATCH."

Jean-Luc Godard

"YOU CAN, YOU SHOULD,
AND IF YOU'RE BRAVE ENOUGH
TO START, YOU WILL."

STEPHEN KING

"COURAGE IS THE ABILITY
TO STAND UP FOR WHAT
YOU BELIEVE IN,
EVEN IF YOU STAND ALONE."

ANONYMOUS

"COURAGE IS ABOUT USING
YOUR BRAIN AND YOUR HEART
WHEN EVERY CELL OF YOUR
BODY IS SCREAMING AT YOU
TO FIGHT OR FLEE."

JIM BUTCHER

"BRAVERY NEVER GOES
OUT OF FASHION."

WILLIAM MAKEPEACE
THACKERAY

"Courage charms us,
because it indicates that
a man loves an idea better
than all things in the
world, that he is thinking
neither of his bed,
nor his dinner, nor his money,
but will venture all to
put in act the invisible
thought of his mind."

RALPH WALDO EMERSON

"ALL BRAVE MEN LOVE;
FOR HE ONLY IS BRAVE WHO
HAS AFFECTIONS TO FIGHT FOR."

NATHANIEL HAWTHORNE

"COURAGE CONSISTS, NOT IN BLINDLY OVERLOOKING DANGER, BUT IN SEEING AND CONQUERING IT."

JEAN PAUL

"We have more respect for a man who robs boldly on the highway, than for a fellow who jumps out of a ditch, and knocks you down behind your back. Courage is a quality so necessary for maintaining virtue, that it is always respected even when it is associated with vice."

SAMUEL JOHNSON

"It is an error to suppose that courage means courage in everything. Most people are brave only in the dangers to which they accustom themselves."

Edward Bulwer-Lytton

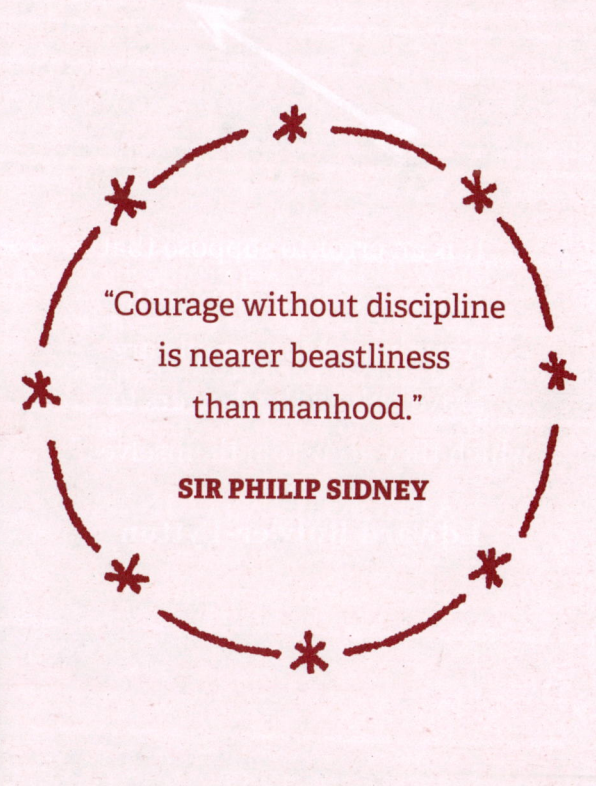

"Courage without discipline
is nearer beastliness
than manhood."

SIR PHILIP SIDNEY

"The world is a dangerous place
to live; not because of the people
who are evil, but because of the people
who don't do anything about it."

ALBERT EINSTEIN

**"IF WE SURVIVE DANGER
IT STEELS OUR COURAGE
MORE THAN ANYTHING ELSE."**

BARTHOLD GEORG NIEBUHR

**"COURAGE IN DANGER
IS HALF THE BATTLE."**

PLAUTUS

"It is courage that vanquishes in war, and not good weapons."

MIGUEL DE CERVANTES

"COURAGE IS THE DETERMINATION
TO LIVE A LIFE TRUE TO YOURSELF,
NOT THE LIFE OTHERS
EXPECT OF YOU."

ANONYMOUS

"THE WOUNDED GLADIATOR
FORSWEARS ALL FIGHTING,
BUT SOON FORGETTING
HIS FORMER WOUND
RESUMES HIS ARMS."

OVID

"A MAN OF COURAGE
IS ALSO FULL OF FAITH."

CICERO

"TELL A MAN THAT
HE IS BRAVE,
AND YOU HELP
HIM BECOME SO."

Thomas Carlyle

"When the will defies fear,
when the heart applauds the brain,
when duty throws the gauntlet down to
fate, when honor scorns to compromise
with death this is heroism."

ROBERT GREEN INGERSOLL

"THE SCARS YOU ACQUIRE
BY EXERCISING COURAGE WILL
NEVER MAKE YOU FEEL INFERIOR."

GIOVANNI BATTISTA CIMA

"COURAGE IS THE FIRST OF HUMAN QUALITIES BECAUSE IT IS THE QUALITY WHICH GUARANTEES THE OTHERS."

ARISTOTLE

"To him that waits all things
reveal themselves, provided
that he has the courage
not to deny, in the darkness,
what he has seen in the light."

COVENTRY PATMORE

"COURAGE CONSISTS NOT IN HAZARDING WITHOUT FEAR, BUT BEING RESOLUTELY MINDED IN A JUST CAUSE."

PLUTARCH

"A great deal of talent is lost in this world for the want of a little courage."

SYDNEY SMITH

"A coward flees backward,
away from new things.
A man of courage
flees forward, in the
midst of new things."

JACQUES MARITAIN

"TO DARE IS TO LOSE ONE'S FOOTING MOMENTARILY. TO NOT DARE IS TO LOSE ONESELF."

SØREN KIERKEGAARD

"THE MAN WHO HAS NEVER
BEEN IN DANGER CANNOT
ANSWER FOR HIS COURAGE."

FRANÇOIS DE LA
ROCHEFOUCAULD

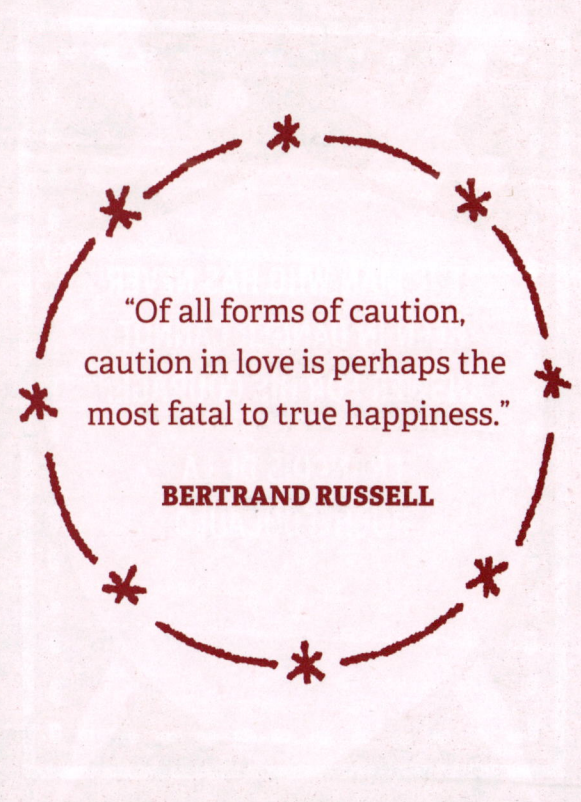

"Of all forms of caution, caution in love is perhaps the most fatal to true happiness."

BERTRAND RUSSELL

"COURAGE IS ADVERSITY'S LAMP."

Luc de Clapiers

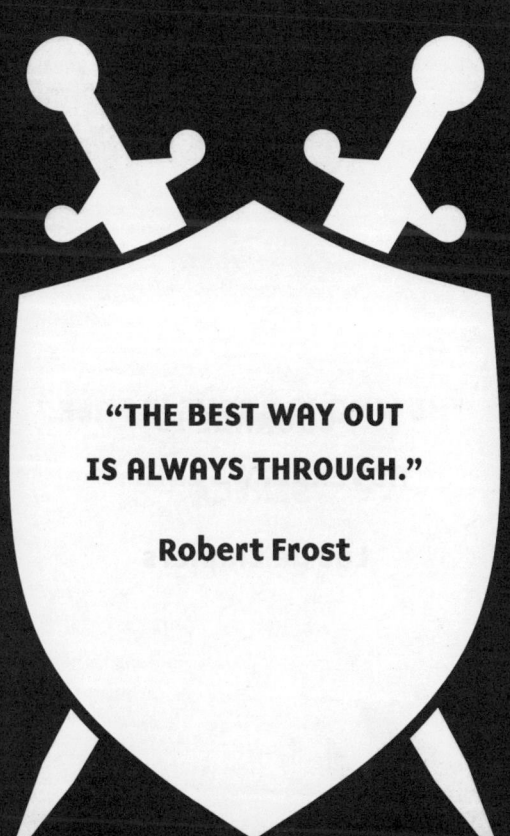

"THE BEST WAY OUT
IS ALWAYS THROUGH."

Robert Frost

"HE WHO IS BRAVE IS FREE."

SENECA

"THE BOLDEST MEASURES
ARE THE SAFEST."

HORATIO NELSON

"Expose yourself to your deepest fear;
after that, fear has no power,
and the fear of freedom shrinks
and vanishes. You are free."

JIM MORRISON

"THE BRAVE MAN CARVES
OUT HIS FORTUNE, AND
EVERYMAN IS THE SUM
OF HIS OWN WORKS."

MIGUEL DE CERVANTES

"COURAGE IS WHAT IT TAKES
TO STAND UP AND SPEAK;
COURAGE IS ALSO WHAT IT TAKES
TO SIT DOWN AND LISTEN."

WINSTON CHURCHILL

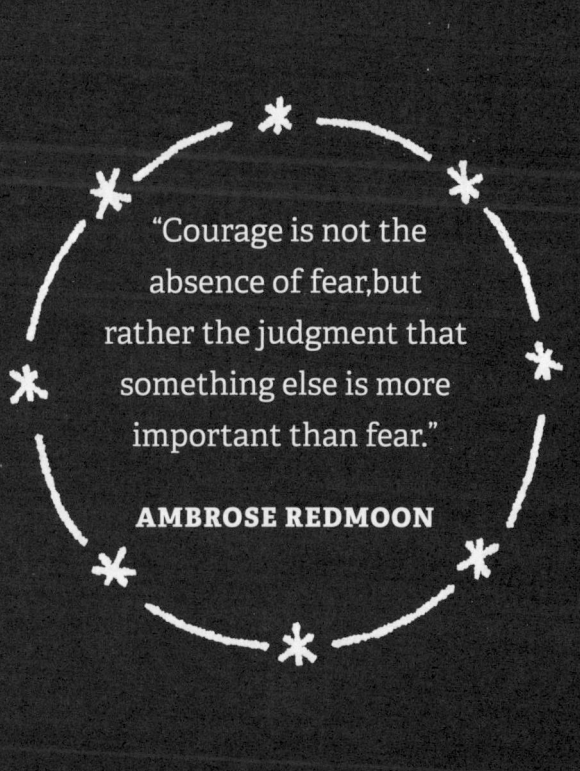

"Courage is not the absence of fear, but rather the judgment that something else is more important than fear."

AMBROSE REDMOON

"DON'T GET DISCOURAGED;
IT IS OFTEN THE LAST KEY IN THE
BUNCH THAT OPENS THE LOCK."

ANONYMOUS

"FIGHT HARD WHEN
YOU ARE DOWN"

JAMES H. WEST

"We don't develop courage
by being happy every day.
We develop it by surviving
difficult times and
challenging adversity."

BARBARA DE ANGELIS

"Courage is never to let
your actions be influenced
by your fears."

ARTHUR KOESTLER

"GOD WILL NOT
HAVE HIS WORK
MADE MANIFEST
BY COWARDS."

RALPH WALDO EMERSON

"I LOVE THE MAN THAT
CAN SMILE IN TROUBLE,
THAT CAN GATHER STRENGTH
FROM DISTRESS, AND GROW
BRAVE BY REFLECTIONS."

THOMAS PAINE

"NEVER LET THE FEAR
OF STRIKING OUT
GET IN YOUR WAY."

BABE RUTH

"A MAN WITHOUT COURAGE
IS TO ME THE MOST DESPICABLE
THING UNDER THE SUN,
A TRAVESTY ON THE WHOLE
SCHEME OF CREATION."

JACK LONDON

"Courage is about learning how
to function despite the fear,
to put aside your instincts to run
or give in completely to the
anger born from fear."

JIM BUTCHER

"LIFE IS MOSTLY FROTH AND BUBBLE; TWO THINGS STAND LIKE STONE, KINDNESS IN ANOTHER'S TROUBLE; COURAGE IN YOUR OWN."

ADAM LINDSAY GORDON

"TRUST THE STILL,
SMALL VOICE THAT SAYS,
'THIS MIGHT WORK AND I'LL TRY IT.'"

DIANE MARIECHILD

"TO LOOK AT SOMETHING AS
THOUGH WE HAD NEVER SEEN IT
BEFORE REQUIRES GREAT COURAGE."

HENRI MATISSE

HOW TO OVERCOME FEAR?

✳ The first step in overcoming fear is to acknowledge its presence and understand its impact on your thoughts and actions. Confront it rather than letting it control you.

✳ Fear often stems from negative beliefs or assumptions. Replace them with positive and empowering thoughts.

✳ Take small, gradual steps outside your comfort zone. Start with manageable challenges that push your boundaries but are still within reach.

✳ Reach out to friends or family members who can provide support and guidance as you face your fears. Their encouragement, advice, and perspective can bolster your confidence.

"Don't be afraid of your fears.
They're not there to scare you.
They're there to let you know
that something is worth it."

C. JOYBELL C.

"LET BRAVERY BE THY CHOICE,
BUT NOT BRAVADO."

MENANDER

"TO UNCOVER YOUR TRUE
POTENTIAL YOU MUST FIRST
FIND YOUR OWN LIMITS
AND THEN YOU HAVE TO
HAVE THE COURAGE TO
BLOW PAST THEM."

PICABO STREET

"Courage is the foundation
of integrity."

KESHAVAN NAIR

"Nothing in life is to be feared,
it is only to be understood.
Now is the time to understand
more, so that we may fear less."

MARIE CURIE

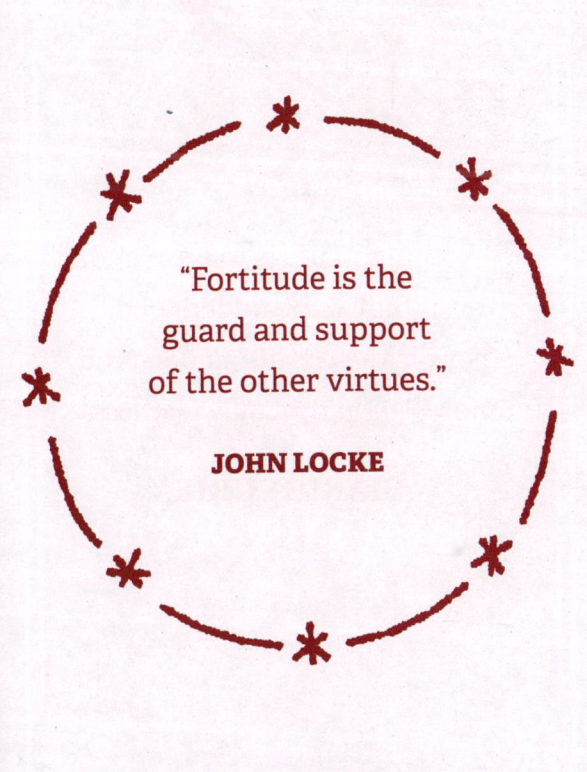

"Fortitude is the
guard and support
of the other virtues."

JOHN LOCKE

"I told myself, Malala,
you have already faced death.
This is your second life.
Don't be afraid.
If you are afraid,
you can't move forward."

MALALA YOUSAFZAI

"I BEG YOU TAKE COURAGE;
THE BRAVE SOUL CAN
MEND EVEN DISASTER."

Catherine the Great

"You gain strength, courage, and confidence by every experience in which you really stop to look fear in the face. You are able to say to yourself, 'I lived through this horror. I can take the next thing that comes along.'"

ELEANOR ROOSEVELT

"COURAGE IS THE LADDER ON WHICH ALL THE OTHER VIRTUES MOUNT."

CLARE BOOTHE LUCE

"TO SHARE YOUR WEAKNESS IS TO MAKE YOURSELF VULNERABLE; TO MAKE YOURSELF VULNERABLE IS TO SHOW YOUR STRENGTH."

CRISS JAMI

"COURAGE IS LOOKING FEAR
RIGHT IN THE EYE AND SAYING,
"GET THE HELL OUT OF MY WAY,
I'VE GOT THINGS TO DO."

ANONYMOUS

"IT TAKES COURAGE TO
EXAMINE YOUR LIFE AND
TO DECIDE THAT THERE ARE
THINGS YOU WOULD LIKE TO
CHANGE, AND IT TAKES
EVEN MORE COURAGE TO
DO SOMETHING ABOUT IT."

SUE HADFIELD

"WITHOUT COURAGE
THERE CANNOT BE TRUTH,
AND WITHOUT TRUTH THERE
CAN BE NO OTHER VIRTUE."

SIR WALTER SCOTT

"FORTUNE ALWAYS FAVORS THE BRAVE, AND NEVER HELPS A MAN WHO DOES NOT HELP HIMSELF."

P. T. Barnum

"THE BEST HEARTS ARE
EVER THE BRAVEST."

LAURENCE STERNE

"SOME TEMPTATIONS ARE
SO GREAT IT TAKES GREAT
COURAGE TO YIELD TO THEM."

OSCAR WILDE

"TRUE STRENGTH IS THE
COURAGE TO ADMIT
OUR WEAKNESSES."

SIMON SINEK

"WE NEED A BACKBONE,
NOT A WISHBONE."

JOYCE MEYER

"CONSCIENCE IS THE ROOT OF ALL TRUE COURAGE; IF A MAN WOULD BE BRAVE LET HIM OBEY HIS CONSCIENCE."

James Freeman Clarke